MW01254764

The Lost Foot Soldiers

Blackballed and Exiled in America

Freddie Mitchell

©2018 Freddie Mitchell
All rights reserved

ISBN 978-1-7320008-1-0

No part of this book may be reproduced, stored
in a retrieval system, or transmitted in any form
or by any means, electronic, mechanical,
photocopying, recording or otherwise without
the written permission of the author.

Published by

Emerge Publishing Group, LLC
Riviera Beach, FL
www.emergepublishers.com
561.601.0349

Freddie Mitchell, 2018
The Lost Foot Soldiers
1. History 2. Civic 3. Civil Rights

Printed in the United States of America

CONTENTS

Dedication

"Dedicated to the Lost Foot Soldiers and their Families"

Willie Barnette	Mr. Henry Haskin, Jr.
Jimmy Booth	Mr. Henry Haskin, Sr.
Rev. Williams M. Branch	Johnny Ray Haskins
Jessis Brown	Sandy Hilton
Threet Brown	Orangette Howard
Wanda Brown	Mr. Violia Howard
Ephiram Byrd	Thomas Hunter
Ned Chandler	Marie Jackson
Tim Chandler	Orazaen Jackson
Mrs. Octiva Chaney	Ervin James
John Dillard	Meg James, Jr.
John Henry Drake	Percy James
John Henry Fitts	Eddie Jones
Mrs. Lena Frost	Joseph Jones
Juanita Gilbert	Eula King
Tommy Gilbvert	Frank King
Rev. Thomas Gilmore	Jessie King
Joe Nathan Grayer	Walter McIntoch
Bobby Harris	Mrs. Alberta Mitchell

Mr. Fred D. Mitchell

Michael Oates

Earnest Perry

Atlas Phillips

Sandy Phillips

Harold Rattiff

Sid Robertson

Glen Samuel

Tommie Samuel

Charie Saulberry

Gen Stallworth

James Taylor

Ella Thomas

Jessie Ware

Rolex Watters

Fred Williams

The Beginning

I Freddie Mitchell, was born April 2, 1951 in Demopolis, Alabama to Fred & Alberta Mitchell. At the age of three months I was given to my grandmother, Mrs. Lula Mitchell, my father's mother.

My earliest remembrance of life was living on the riverfront, in a community called Gritty. Around the age of nine, the city jailhouse was across the street from our house. My grandmother used to sell whiskey and food plates to the inmates in jail. I was the runner to the jailhouse and back. There was one white store in the community called Terrance Bait Shop.

My grandmother and I traveled to Detroit very often. We stayed two or three years at a time. My first remembrance about Detroit was as a young boy from the south. I had to fight and prove that coming from the south didn't make me less of a person. The street we lived on was Commonwealth, between 14th and 12th, cross by Warren Avenue on the corner of Warren and 14th, the world famous Twenty Grand Ballroom where all of Motown stars appear weekly.

I remember one day my uncle, James Mitchell, whom we lived with, sent me to the store on Warren. On the way to the store, I was confronted by two young boys. They asked my name and where I was from. I didn't know I wasn't supposed to talk to them. I was almost to the store when they jumped me, took my money, and ran. So I went back home and my uncle asked "Where are the items I told you to get from the store?" I said, "I got jumped and the boys took my money." So, James pulled out this big thick belt, which he was good with, and told me I had two choices–to either go back and get his money or take this whipping from him. That wasn't a hard choice

I would fight ten guys before settling for a whipping from him. So I went back to the store where the boys were. I guess they were waiting on someone else to jump. They saw me coming and approached me saying "Give us more money."

Unknowing to them I had a small baseball bat. I attacked them and got my money and their's and took the things I bought at the store back home. I was given the lesson about not letting anyone take anything from me. I have been fighting ever since.

We then moved down the street on 14th and from 14th to around the corner, on Hudson Street. I attended Gold Bery Elementary School on Terry and 12th.

Our next move was on Wreford Street and Lindwood. I attended McMichael Middle School located on the campus of Northwestern High School on Grand Blvd., down the street from Motown Studio. Detroit was jumping hard. It was like being in heaven compared to Alabama.

My last year in school in Detroit will never be forgotten. One day during last period class about 2:00 in the afternoon, the school started buzzing through out. Teachers, kids, everyone was hollering and crying. It was then announced over the intercom that President Kennedy has been shot in Dallas, Texas. Later, it was announced that President John F. Kennedy was dead. He was killed by a sniper while riding in a motorcade. He was shot down. It was a day that will forever remain in my mind. A date never to be forgotten, November 22, 1963.

My grandmother and my aunt Irdelia Foster lived on Front Street, a couple of doors down the street from my parents and seven brothers and sisters. My father was a Korea War Vet and worked for the Webbs at a cotton gin. He attended college on the G.I. Bill in Eutav, Alabama.

On Friday nights, we watched the Friday Night fights on TV. Together, my first viewing of a color TV was a piece of plastic that went over the TV screen. It had three colors to it. It had a wide orange, green and yellow strips; your color was the three colored strips. They would go down the street a couple of doors down from the house to Ms. Mattie Robertson house and pay a quarter to watch TV on Saturday, cartoon day.

Then we moved on Capital Street across from Mr. Robert Jones and family. One night after the fight my daddy took me home in his car. He told me that he didn't have much gas to cut the car off, so that when he slowed down to jump out of the car, which I did, not thinking about the car was faster than me. I hit the ground pretty hard and got scared up.

At work my daddy was the night watchman; also, he had to make rounds every hour on the hour and had a clock that he carried around with him. Located in different parts of the warehouse was different keys to punch the clock at every location. If the clock was not punched every hour, it would show up the hours you missed. So daddy started taking me with him to learn where the keys were so that I could make some rounds for him and he could get some sleep.

We stayed in a one room shack about the size of a small bathroom, with an Army lot, and a small wood heater. The summer of 64 in Detroit, a friend of my uncle's called Shorty Man, whose name was Delton Barnes, bought me a three speed bike. At that time they were called Skinny Mitchells. So I bought it back to Alabama with me. We lived on Fulton Street between Mr. Silas James and Rev. Oliver Brown and his grandson, George Brown, Jr., whom we called Huckabuck. Huck was a collector of pigeons.

The beginning of 1965, I had my bike. I got a job carrying newspapers. I had my own route for a while. Somehow a white guy ended up with the whole town under him. So I worked with him

One day after raining all night, a really bad thunderstorm poured down rain. His brother showed up so we could drive the route. He didn't get out of the car at all. I had to throw papers on my side and his side. I was soaking wet and he was powder dry. So I started shorting the route. Just getting the one on my side. He didn't know the route, so we missed some customers. The next day the manager was back. As soon as he picked me up and we had worked about ten minutes, he started hollering and cussing about people not getting their paper yesterday. Then all of a sudden he slaps me and grabs me in the collar talking about missed papers.

I was thirteen years old, so I was swollen up with anger. I threw a few more papers. We came to a house where I had to get out of the car and put the paper in the screen door. That was fifty years ago, and we haven't seen each other since.

I kept going on a shortcut home and told him to f--k him and the newspapers. That is when reality set in. I had no one to tell. For if I told my daddy about it, it was going to be a bad ending because white people could make blacks disappear without any questions. That caused my anger and resentment toward white people to become deep rooted from that moment on. In fifty years I never told anyone about what happened until now.

"Three hundred years of humiliation, abuse

and deprivation cannot be expected to

find voice in a whisper."

Martin Luther King Jr.

Protests and
Sit-Ins

The later part of 1964 black people in Dempolis began to realize how far the opposing Civil Rights was being cast aside. S.N.C.C. had found their way to town to organize people to vote and to get them registered.

Rev. Richard Boone, James Orange, Rev. Webb and Rev. Andrew Marrisette started having Mass meeting to form a plan of action. The police

and Chief Cooper, Sgt. Johnson and Officer
Charles McCrey started following the workers
around town. We were holding mass meetings at
the Old Morning Star Baptist Church across the
street from U.S. Jones High School. The city all
blacks where we students attended school. The
leader started to organize sit-ins and boycott
downtown at the stores.

Old Morning Star Baptist Church

U.S. Jones High School

The people who participated in the sit-in and boycotted was arrested taken to jail. About that time S.C.L.C. came to help out. They started protest marches to protest the arrests and the rights to be seated and served. On the day of the march, every police, state trooper, sheriff and any white man who wanted to whip heads showed up and was issued tear gas and billy clubs to use on us marchers.

The plan was to march down to the jail house on the other side of town, where city hall was also located. During the first march, we were attacked leaving off the church grounds with tear gas. The next time after about four blocks, long enough to stretch out the line of marches away from the church, we were blocked off and confronted by the force of evil. We were stopped by police Chief Copper and confronted at the corner of Cedar and Jackson Street. We were told that this was an unlawful assembly and we had five minutes to disburse. So following our training, we sang freedom songs and sat down on the ground.

Jackson Street

Meanwhile, the police were putting on gas masks and tighten billy clubs while laughing. Soon they started throwing tear gas and tried to surround the marchers to cut off any escape route. So we laid down on the ground and balled up in a knot to protect ourselves. They started beating and kicking us. We would take much as we could. We started picking up the tear gas and throwing back at them, fighting them back and running back to the church. They ran and chased us. Once at the church we licked our wounds, found out who was hurt, and who they took off to jail and who was missing. The police surrounded the church so no one could get in or out.

We regrouped, started singing and having mass meetings all over. The next day, the protest began again. We slipped out of church two or three times to go home. The student that left school was not permitted to step on the school campus and was expelled.

A couple of days later we tried to march again. This time we traveled the same route, but the police let us continue to march to the jail house and stopped us again in front of the jail and told us the same thing.

"This is an unlawful assembly and you have five minutes to disburse." So once again, we sat down and covered up. They started tear gassing, beating and chasing us. I lived one block from the jail house, so I tried to reach home; it was a mass confusion. The police chased me home and I ran into the house. When I closed the door behind me I heard two loud bangs and the house shook. Smoke started to fill up the house with me and my grandmother in the house. So we put wet rags over our faces. After the smoke cleared, we realized the police had blown up my grandmother front porch,

living room and destroyed my new bike. We lived

between Mr. Silas James and Rev. Oliver Brown

on Fulton and Strawberry Street.

We went back to the church and regrouped again. The police started picking people up putting them in jail. They came by my mom and Dad house and told them that if they didn't keep out of that mess, something was going to happen. We still continued to hold mass meetings.

Dr. King was coming to Demopolis at the request of the local S.C.L.C. Leader Henry Haskins, Jr. We planned another march with the same results.

"By the force of our demands, our determination
and our numbers, we shall splinter the
segregated South into a thousand pieces and
put them back together in the image of
God and democracy."

John Lewis

"There's no problem on the planet that can't be solved without violence. That is the lesson of the civil rights movement."

Andrew Young

Jail

I was arrested along with fifty or sixty more people, mostly children and students from school. The city jail was already full. So us kids who were under sixteen years old were transfered to the county jail. Everyone sixteen and over was sent to Camp Thomaston, an ex-German prison. They cut us off from the outside. They arrested my father for not keeping me out of the movement and sent him to Camp Thomaston. I

Old Police Station

was sent to the county jail in Linda, Alabama. They put about ten people in a four man cell. We took turns sleeping on a concrete floor. We hardly had room to move around. The conditions were worse than worse. The fed us for breakfast, a hard biscuit, so hard if you threw it on the floor it bounced back up, a strip of salty fatback meat, and yellow grits that were turned yellow by adding salt peter, something to kill your nature, and a cup of coffee. We would get potatoes different ways twice a day. Everyday, we had open commode, where we had to drink water out of the top of the commode tank. They hid us out so no one could get in touch with us.

I remember Atlas Phillip and Willie Barnette were in the same cell. No shower, bed or wash bowl. Imagine the odor with every cell packed with kids all under sixteen. It was dark except a light that shine thru a small window and creaks in the wall. The big four-hundred pound jailer named Jimmy walked the hall with an oversized ring of keys that rattled when he walked, so you could hear him coming all over the cell block. After being held in jail for a month, Dr. King had come and gone, yet we still had the jails and the prison easily full.

The police slowed down arresting people who were still marching because thy didn't have anywhere to put them. So we got out of jail after Bloody Sunday.

The next week on Saturday, we made it back to Demopolis and went straight to the church where people were loading up in anything that ran. We headed to Selma for the start of the march. During the sixties the State of Alabama was the most physical, vicious, segregated state in the United States, led by the City of Birmingham, Alabama with their King pin Sheriff Bill Conner, the devil himself.

Selma came next on the list and the fifty miles that we were about to walk was known as the Most Dangerous Fifty Miles in the World for blacks. Fifty miles out in the open where Hills and Valleys with tree-lined streets and bushes on each side. We marched right down the middle..

They shouted at us, threw things at us. We were steady walking and signing, trying to make our ten miles a day so we could camp out and eat and get off the highway. And in the night began entertainment by the top movie star actors, entertainers from all over the World.

"Justice is never given; it is exacted and the struggle must be continuous for freedom is never a final fact, but a continuing evolving process to higher and higher levels of human, social, economic, political and religious relationship."

Asa Philip Randolph

"Truth is powerful and it prevails."

Sojourner Truth

"I have learned over the years that when one's mind is made up, this diminishes fear; knowing what must be done does away with fear"

Rosa Parks

The Lost Foot Soldiers

At our time in life, when our name was called,
we set out on a march to bring Justice for All.

We marched through the valley of the shadow of death,
step by step; we never stopped for rest.

Ten miles a day, we march on our way, singing our freedom songs,
praying that God had us in His arms.

From all walks of life we came,
marching for freedom not trying to make a name.

Surrounded by death on each and every side
we continued to march, never getting tired.

We came young and old, black and white
for we knew we had to finish this fight.

Fifty miles we went down the road,
never thinking about life's toll.

We answered the call from above
to offer our life for brotherly love.

We showed the world what we could do,
staying united to see the march through.

Without the foot soldiers, who answered the call and came,
The world might have known the man called Dr. KING!

Written By
Freddie Mitchell
Demopolis, Alabama

50th Anniversary Bridge Crossing Jubilee
March 7, 2015
Foot Soldier Breakfast
50

The Walk

Through the

Valley

The march started out from Brown Chapel Church. The sight of all the people and police dogs was a sight to behold for a thirteen year old. We were surrounded by people, black and white from all walks of life, every shape, form and fashion. We were headed to Montgomery, Alabama, the State Capital. A city that fifty miles east of Selma on Highway 80. We were marching and singing Freedom songs. We marched on the left side of Highway 80 East. The traffic was reduced to two lanes on the right side with State Troopers and National Guardsmans, and photographers in between us.

There were white people mixed in with them, hollering, cussing, shouting, "niggers, kill niggers" and everything else that they could think of to say. We marched ten miles a day stopping at the end of the day to a campsite that was prepared before we got there. We lined up to get our plate to eat, we found us a place to sleep on the ground.

After everyone had gotten settled in we enjoyed the concert with different stars, such as Peter, Paul and Mary, Sammie Davis, Jr, Michael London, Dick Gregory, Tony Bennett, Samaui Parkes Jr, Cher, Red Foxx, Lena Horne, Harry

Bellefonte, Sidney Poitier and many more. Each night we had different cast, Dr. King was seated on the ground in front of the stage. He was surrounded by children sitting around like the old story tellers in a village. We were out in the pasture in the dark not knowing who or what was in the bushes and trees behind the lights. At that moment in time we were too young to be afraid. This was major blackness on the move. Here we are marching as a whole for freedom going up against the major power structure of America.

We were prepared for whatever happened, the scene was something like in a dream. All of the world leaders for peace were among us and we all mixed in like family. The next four days was a repeat of the first. Walking and singing toward Montgomery.

On our arrival we marched to the campus of St. Jude High School where we camped out for the night and held mass meetings and prayer for a safe trip. The next day we marched to the State capital building where we held a rally. We listened to a host of speakers with Dr. King being the main speaker. We were dismissed to go back to the church and mass meeting late into the night with people leaving out to get back to Selma.

There was a white civil rights worker from Detroit named Viola Luizzo, whom was a volunteer, to take people back and forth. On her last trip with a couple of black kids in the car with her, they were attacked on Highway 80 and killed by the Klu Klux Klan. So we became extra careful, for we were still under attacks.

We got back to Selma the next day. Finally we made it back to Demopolis where protesters sit in and voter drives were still active, and we had more work still ahead of us.

"If you're not angry, you're either a stone, or you're too sick to be angry. You should be angry. You must not be bitter. Bitterness is like cancer. It eats upon the host. It doesn't do anything to the object of its displeasure. So use that anger, yes. You write it. You paint it. You dance it. You march it. You vote it. You do everything about it. You talk it. Never stop talking it."

Maya Angelou

"Democracy is a method of realizing the
broadest measure of justice to all human beings
... only by putting power in the hands of each
inhabitant can we hope to approximate in the
ultimate use of that power the greatest good to
the greatest number."

W.E.B. Du Bois

The After
Effects

fter the Selma March was over Demopolis became a main topic. S.N.C.C, Scope and S.C.L.C had been in town before Bloody Sunday. The preacher and other supposed leading citizens listing to the leadership of Henry Haskins, Jr.

We had a march downtown led by Hasing, Rev. Richard Boone and Andrew Marrisette where at least 100 more people were arrested. The school was boycotted because those of us students, who marched was kicked out of school for taking part in the movements. A boycott of the businesses was called for. After the movement Demopolis lost twenty-five of its population. Black people were being black balled from any jobs and the students were flunked and had to repeat the same grade the next year.

S.C.L.C. had a strategy that its goes into a place and get the leadership that is already there to back them and their plan. They created a crisis that will bring the press and the media into town. Then Dr. King comes in at the height of the crisis to a head. He don't stay there afterward, and don't come before until the town is ready to explode.

In Demopolis the trouble with the plan was the local failure, but national success. People lost their jobs, got evicted and so on. We were left with case pending in the court system. Demopolis was like Selma, a lot of people were disgusted with the movement. We felt like we had been left holding the bag. We were asking where is Dr. King now. The battle was won nationally, but not on the local level.

The confrontation in Demopolis and Selma had been the work of S.N.C.C.. They were in Demopolis at least a year before S.C.L.C.. It was said that S.C.L.C. moved in and stole the show from S.N.C.C..

Mrs. Lena Frost called for a new round of mass meetings at Petty Memorial Church on North Ash. After about two weeks, a grocery store hired its first black cashiers, and instantly the store filled up with black customers.

Petty Memorial Church

The movement in Demopolis wasn't as healthy as it had been when the summer had open. Because people in the movement were beginning to run out of town leaving the movement to the local weaklings. We continue to boycott the stores and staged sit-in in local stores. Rumor started that the movement was beginning to sell out to the white businesses over in Demopolis.

An article came out in Jet Magazine to the effect of a boycott in rural Alabama was bought out. Some guy named John Israel showed up at a business meeting being held by the businessmen and told them that for Five Thousand Dollars he could put an end to the boycott. It was said they agreed to pay three thousand dollars to put an end to the boycott. The family of the marchs were scorned not only the whites but by the blacks also, who were still afraid of what was going to happen when S.N.C.C. and S.C.L.C. left town.

A lady named Mrs. Viola Howard ran a boarding house and nursing home for blacks. Most of the freedom fighters stayed there. Mrs. Howard

Mrs. Viola Howard Old Folks Nursing Home

had a daughter named Orangette, who was 14 years old, who marched from Selma to Montgomery. Her job was to march with a blind white man and Joe also along with the one legged white guy. She and her mom after the march was being harassed along with the rest of us who still remained in Demopolis.

I remember one time that the police stopped and picked her up and told her she was being arrested for robbing a grocery store. She denied the charges and was sentenced to one year and a day. This store was one of the stores we boycotted. They sent her to Tutuiden, in Wetumpka, Alabama and she was pregnant at that time and had her baby there. Then the city of Demopolis built a nursing home and took all of her patients and closed down her place and offered her a job working for them with a smile on their face. They fell back into their normal "yes sir" and "no sir" practices and accepted whatever the whites did or told them to do.

There were some token jobs given out and hand picked so called black leader to represent us. They are controlled by the white power structure. We finally got a police chief and a couple of black officers. A couple of hand picked city councilmen. Until this day the City of Demopolis, after all we went through, still remains an oreo cookie city, where nothing is said or done on behalf of the blacks. Because the blacks never complained about anything, they are still controlled by whites to this day. All of the marches were run out of the City never to return. Nobody cares or even said anything about it. What happened or what is happening now?

Just one more event that they tried to be sweep under the rug. The 1966 census said that Maring Co. meaning Demopolis had lost twenty-five percent of blacks from the spring of 1965 who once lived there.

Because of our efforts and sacrifice the successful passing of the National Voters Rights Bill. Blacks were elected to positions for the firt time in history. Neighboring county, Greene County elected the first black probate Judge Rev. William Branch and the first black sheriff, Rev., Thomas Gilmore. The fruits of all our labor was election of the first black President Barack Obama in history.

Where did the Foot Soldiers go?

"Civil rights are civil rights. There are no persons who are not entitled to their civil rights. We have to recognize that we have a long way to go, but we have to go that way together."

Dorothy Height

"Change will not come if we wait for some

other person or some other time. We are

the one's we've been waiting for. We are the

change that we seek."

Former President Barack Obama

I would like to dedicate my award, "THE CONGRESSIONAL GOLD MEDAL" which is the highest award that the United States can give to a citizen to the following people:

- My father, Mr. Fred Michell, RIP who during the civil rights movement of 1965, in Demopolis, Alabama was arrested by the Demopolis Police and taken to the city jail where he was later transfered to the State of Alabama Prison Camp, Camp Thomaston, located in Thomaston, FL. He was held there for over a month. He was arrested for my actions in the movement. Since I was only 13 years old, he was held responsible for me.

- To my mother, Mrs. Albert Mitchell, who took an active part in the boycotting and sitting-in protest that took place in Demopolis.

- My Grandmother, Mrs. Lula Mitchell, who raised me from the age of 3 months old along with my 10 brothers and sisters.

- My family, and to the families of The Lost FOOT SOLDIERS who where ever they might be!!!

One Love!!

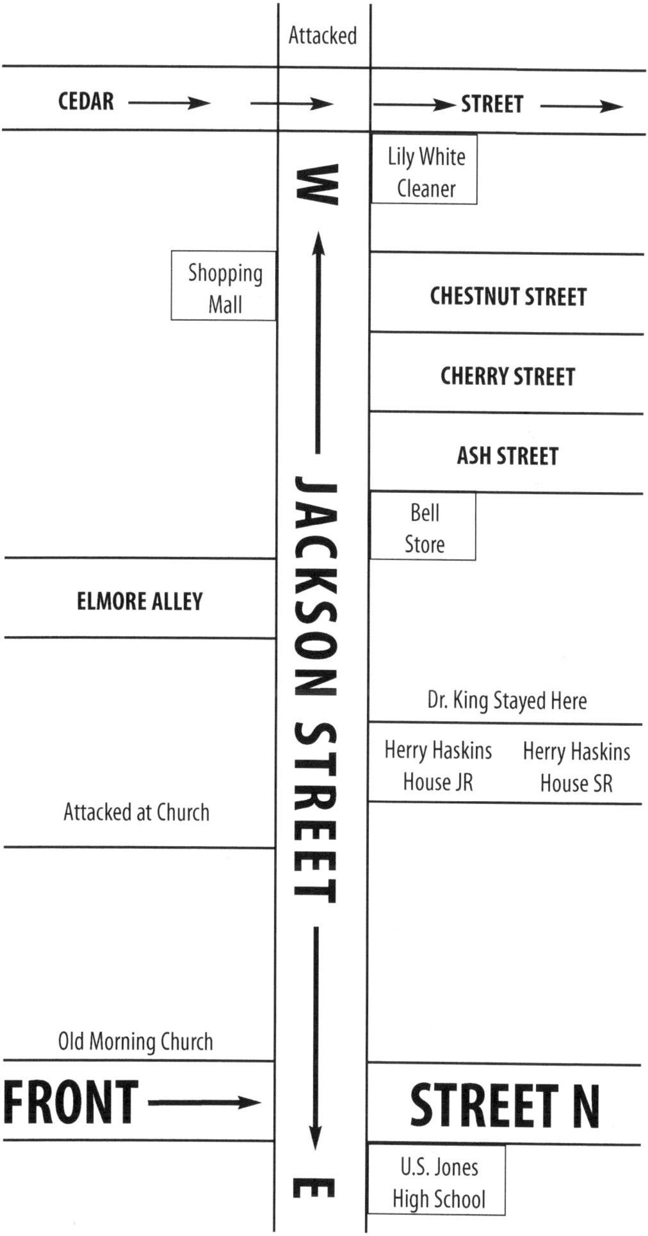
Attacked
CEDAR
STREET
Lily White Cleaner
W
Shopping Mall
CHESTNUT STREET
CHERRY STREET
ASH STREET
Bell Store
JACKSON STREET
ELMORE ALLEY
Dr. King Stayed Here
Herry Haskins House JR
Herry Haskins House SR
Attacked at Church
Old Morning Church
FRONT
STREET N
E
U.S. Jones High School

Tear Gas
Blowed Porch Up
At My House

City
Hall
Attack

WALNUT STREET

Movie
Theater

City
Hall

STRAWBERRY STREET

Craw
Nutty

WASHINGTON STREET

Jones
Auto

CEDAR STREET

Frog Bottom

Loyad

Jane's House

WALNUT STREET

CAPTILAL STREET

LYON STREET

MONROE STREET

FULTON STREET

CHERRY STREET

Black Nursing Home
'Dr. King Hid Out

Brick Yard

ASH STREET

REFTY
MERKER

LENA
FROST

About the Author
Freddie James Mitchell

I was born in Demopolis, Alabama April 2, 1951. I joined the Civil rights movement at a very young age. In 1955 at the age of thirteen, I became a foot soldier. I was introduced to the movement by the Student Nonviolent coordinating committee (S.N.C.C.). S.D.C.C. was in Demopolis for the purpose of organizing a voter registration drive. I would help by going around town trying to get blacks registered to vote.

A little later the Southern Christian Leadership Conference made its way to Demopolis. They provided training on nonviolent tactics that were used during the boycotts, sit-ins, and protests that were being held against white businesses.

I and other young students decided to leave school to participate in the movement. Because of that decision, we were expelled from school.

Several times we tried to march from the church to the courthouse downtown. Each time, we were stopped, beaten, and tear-gassed by the local police.

By the age of thirteen, I had been arrested three or four times. The last time we were approached by the police we were sent to jail. Children under the age of 16 were sent to the County Jail in Linden, AL. The ones over 16 were sent to Prison Camp Thomaston in Thomaston, FL. The living conditions at both sites were unbearable for us all. We stayed at these sites for about a month.

After being released from the Merengo County Jail and the German Prison Camp, we went back to the church in Demopolis. We jumped on the back of a truck and headed to Selma. We had not even been home after our release. Once we made it to Selma to join the march, the rest became history. All adults from Demopolis that participated in the march lost their jobs, including my father.

All the students were expelled from school until the following year. That caused us to repeat that same grade for a second year. I am constantly reminded of these times each and every day. I will remember this for the rest of my life. My family will remember as well. For they too helped pay the price. To this day, the struggle goes on.

Made in the USA
Columbia, SC
17 August 2022

64870331R00037